The

Prick

Ways

Phenomenal Swear Word To Color

For Stress Releasing

J.N. Moorcroft

Happy Coloring!

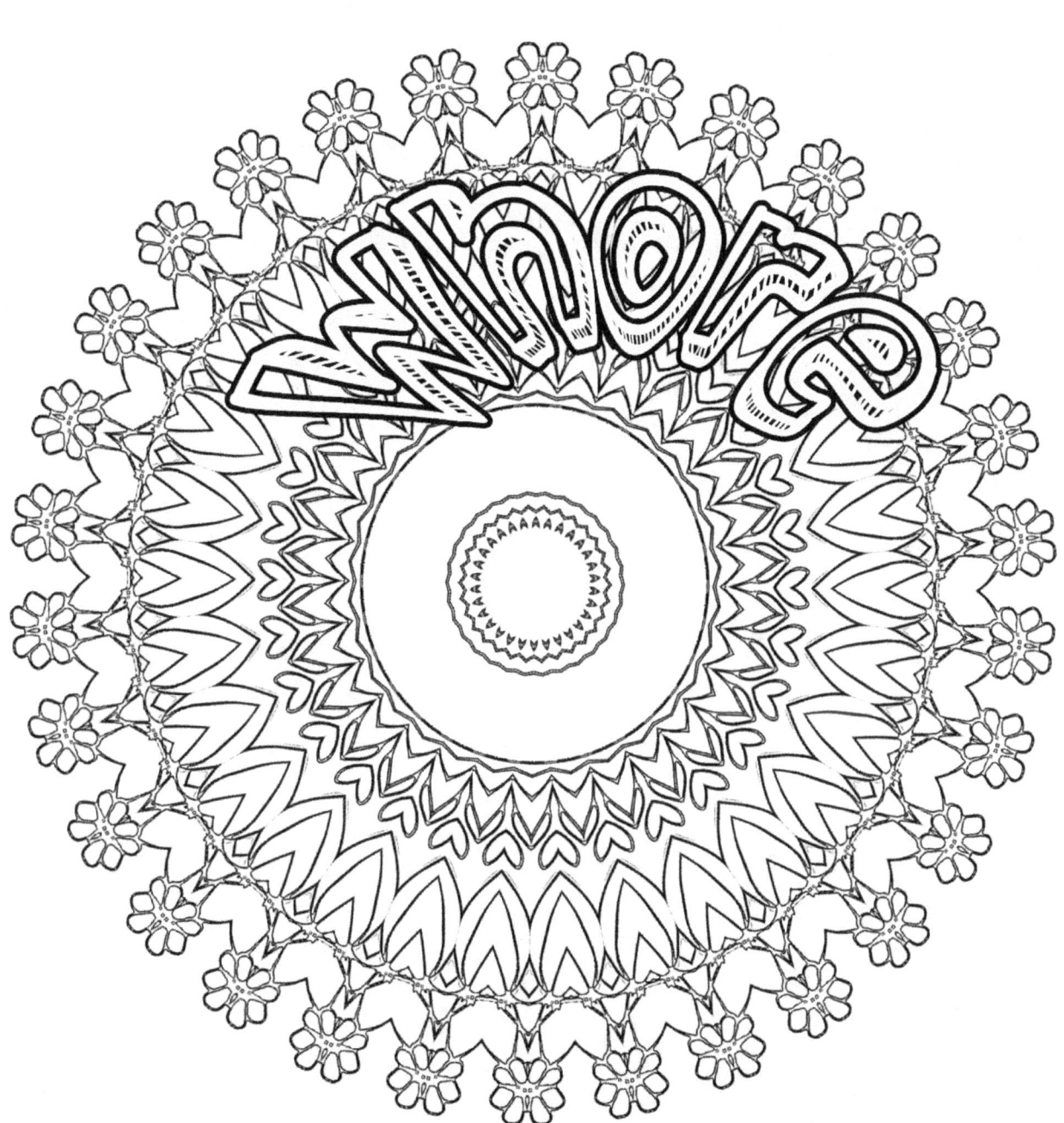

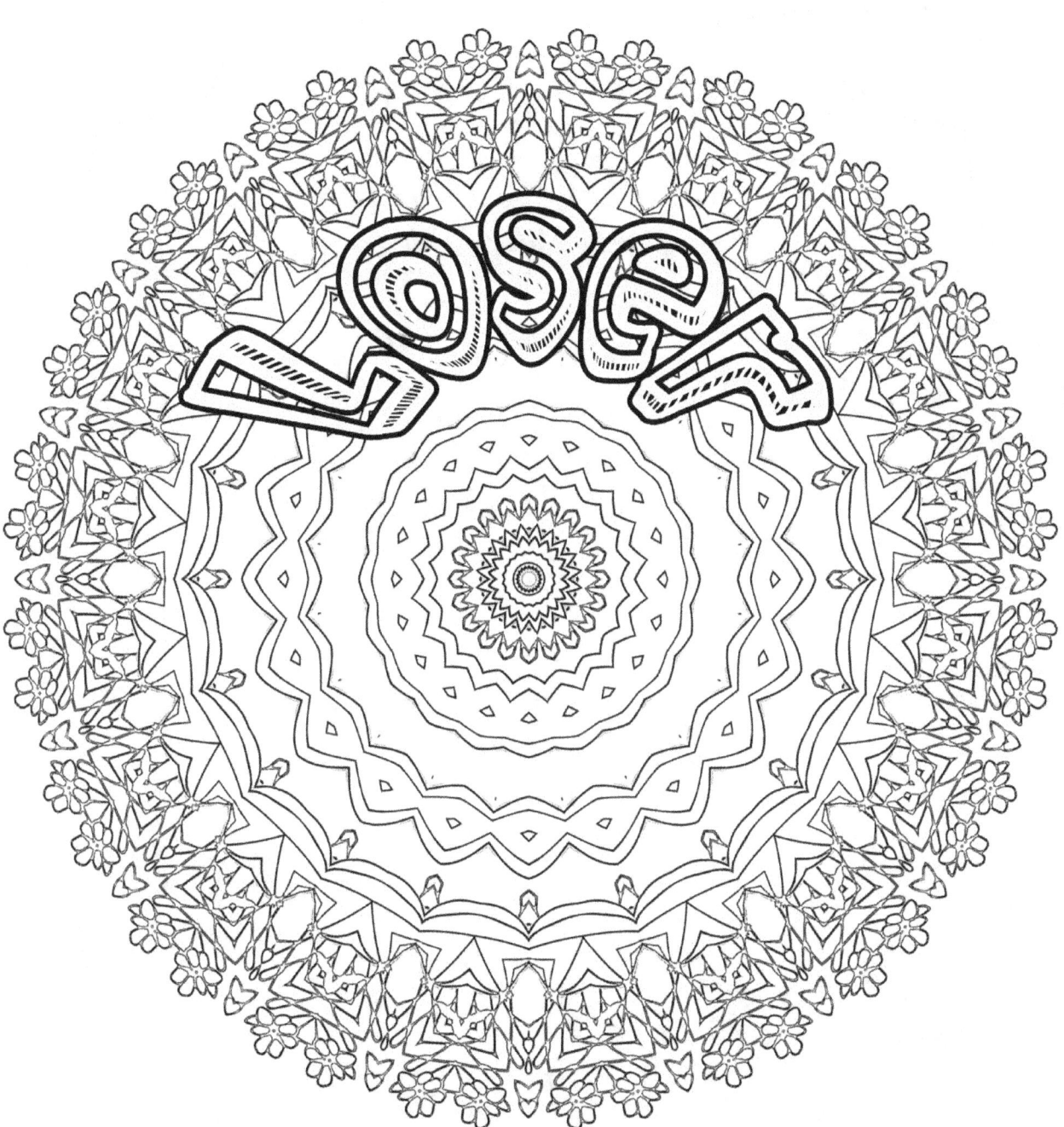

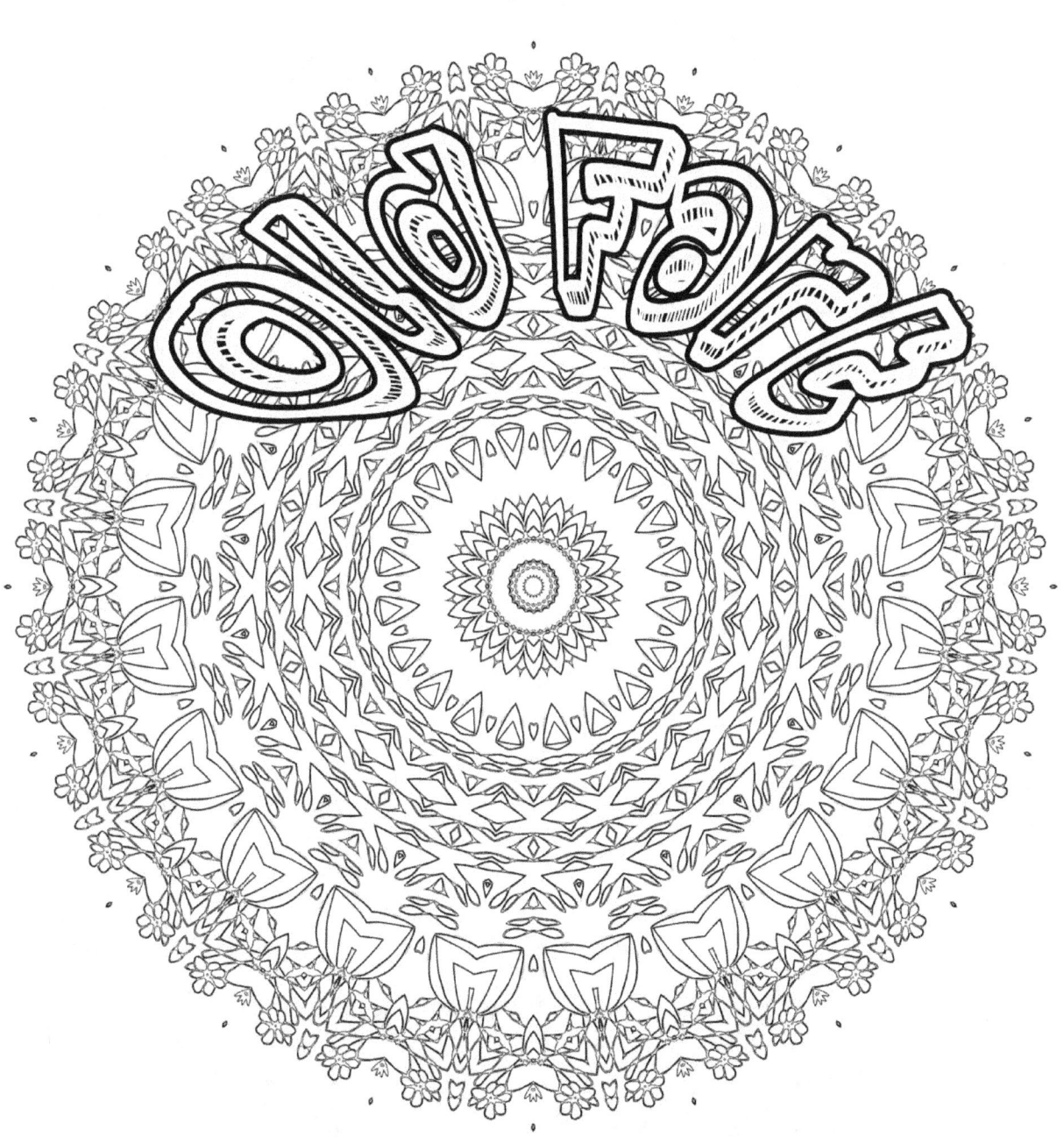

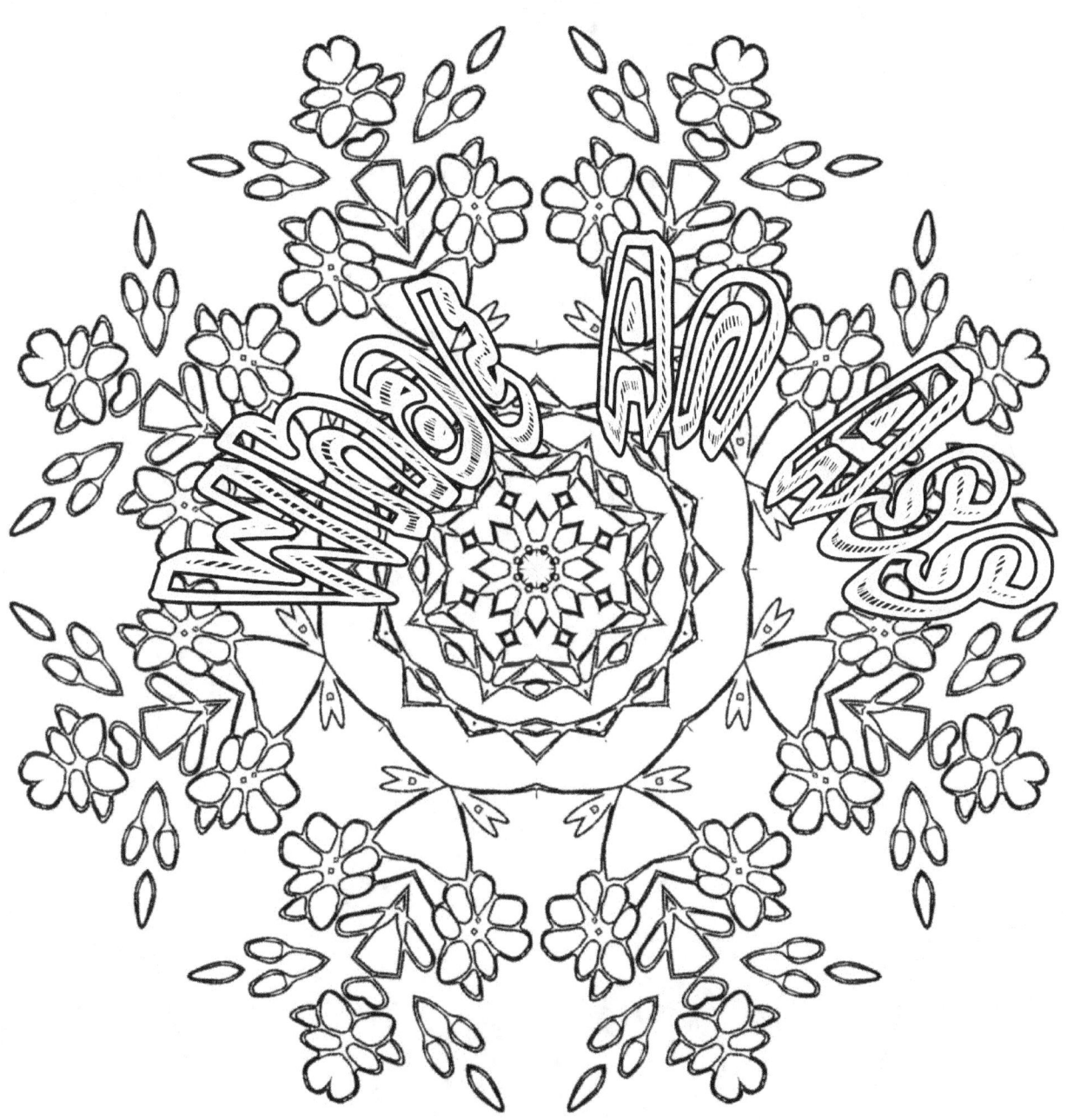

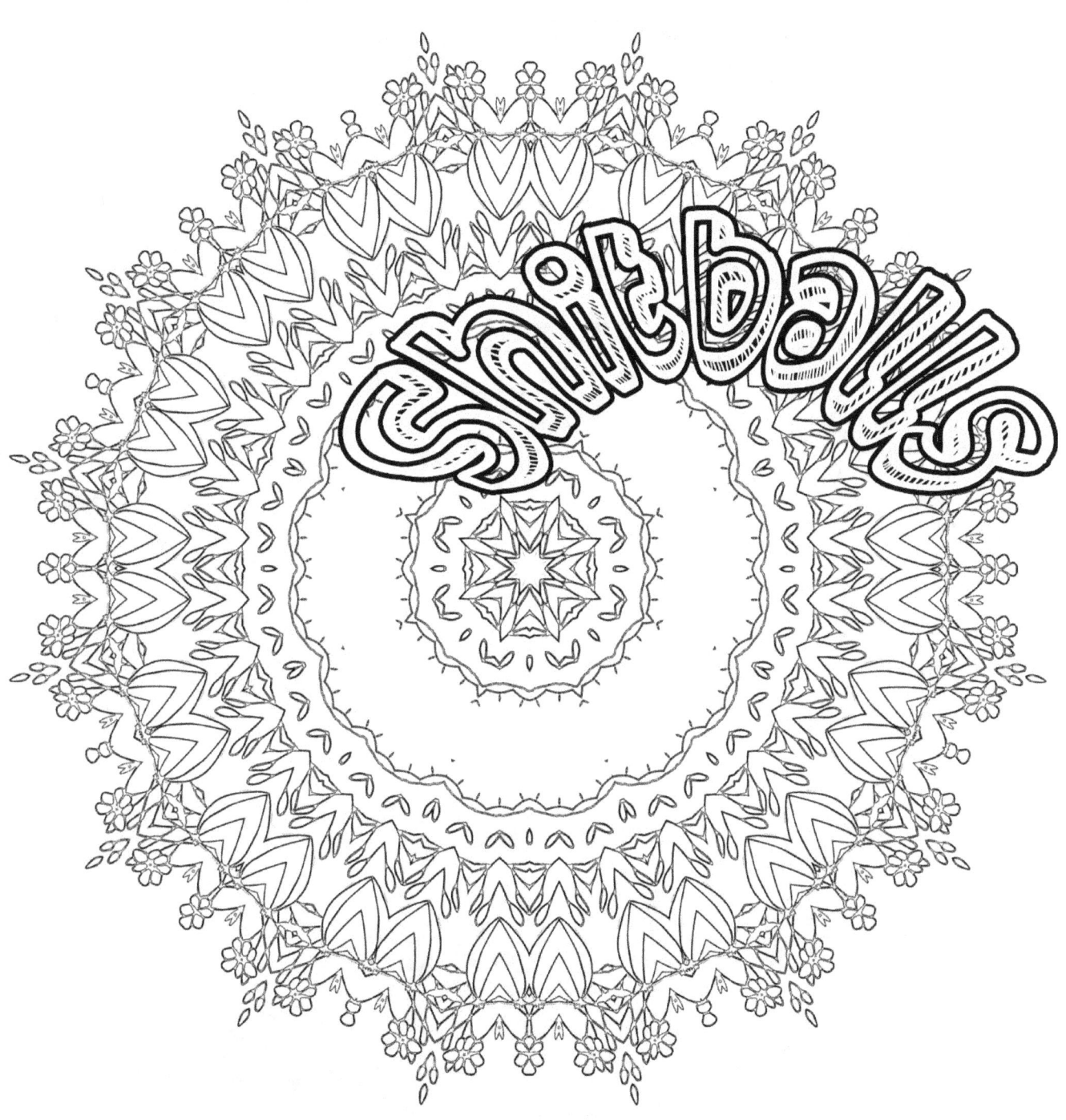

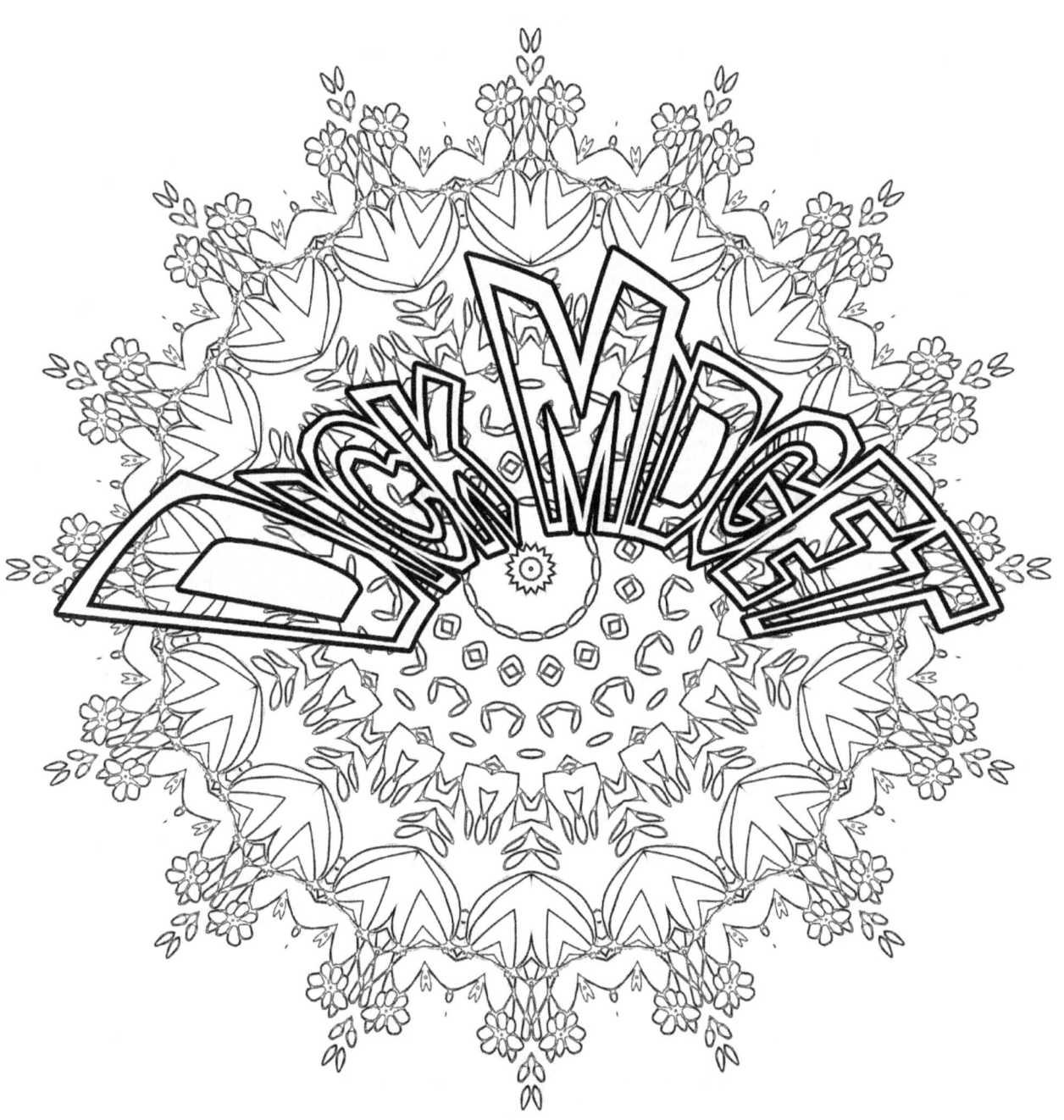

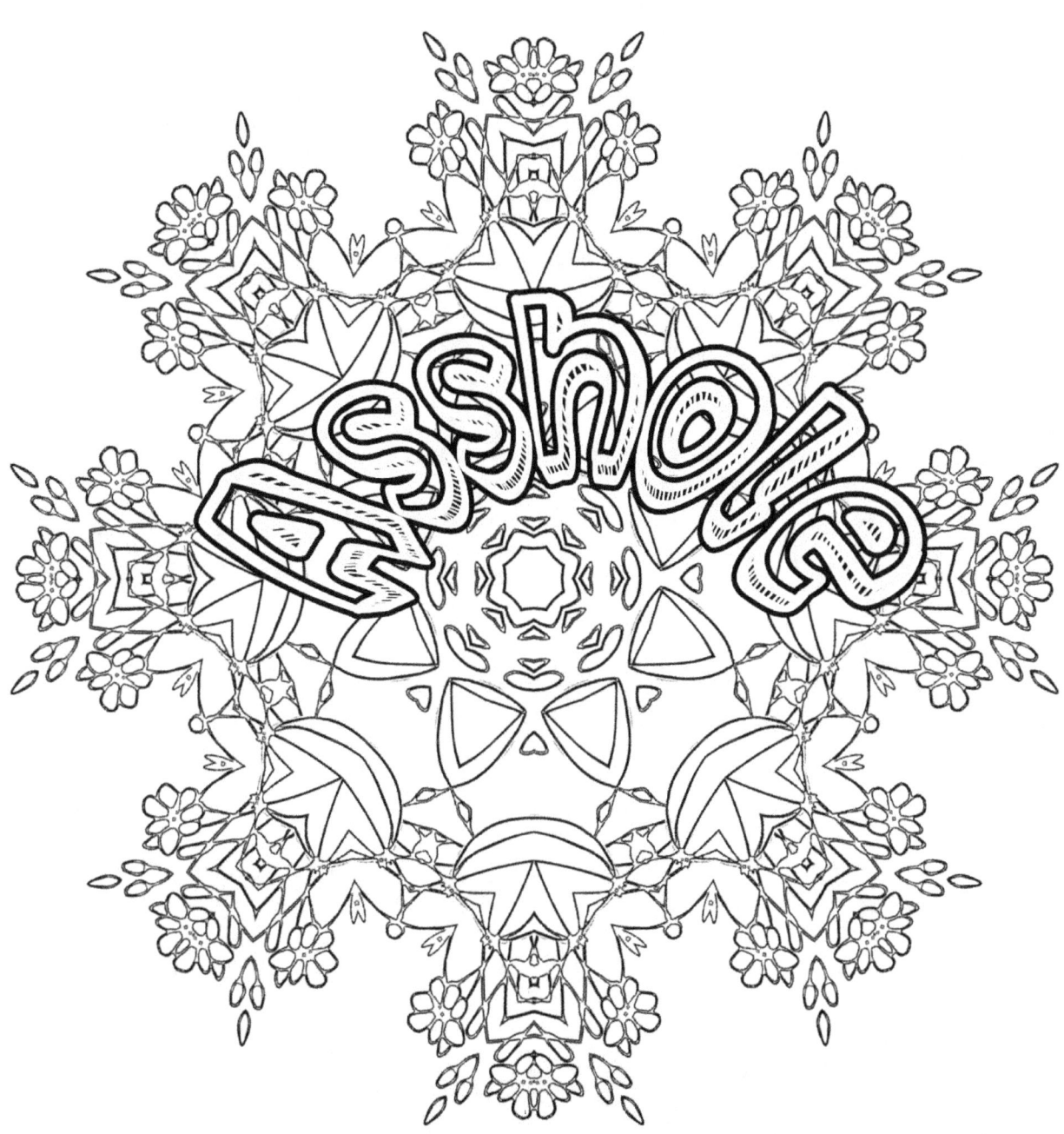

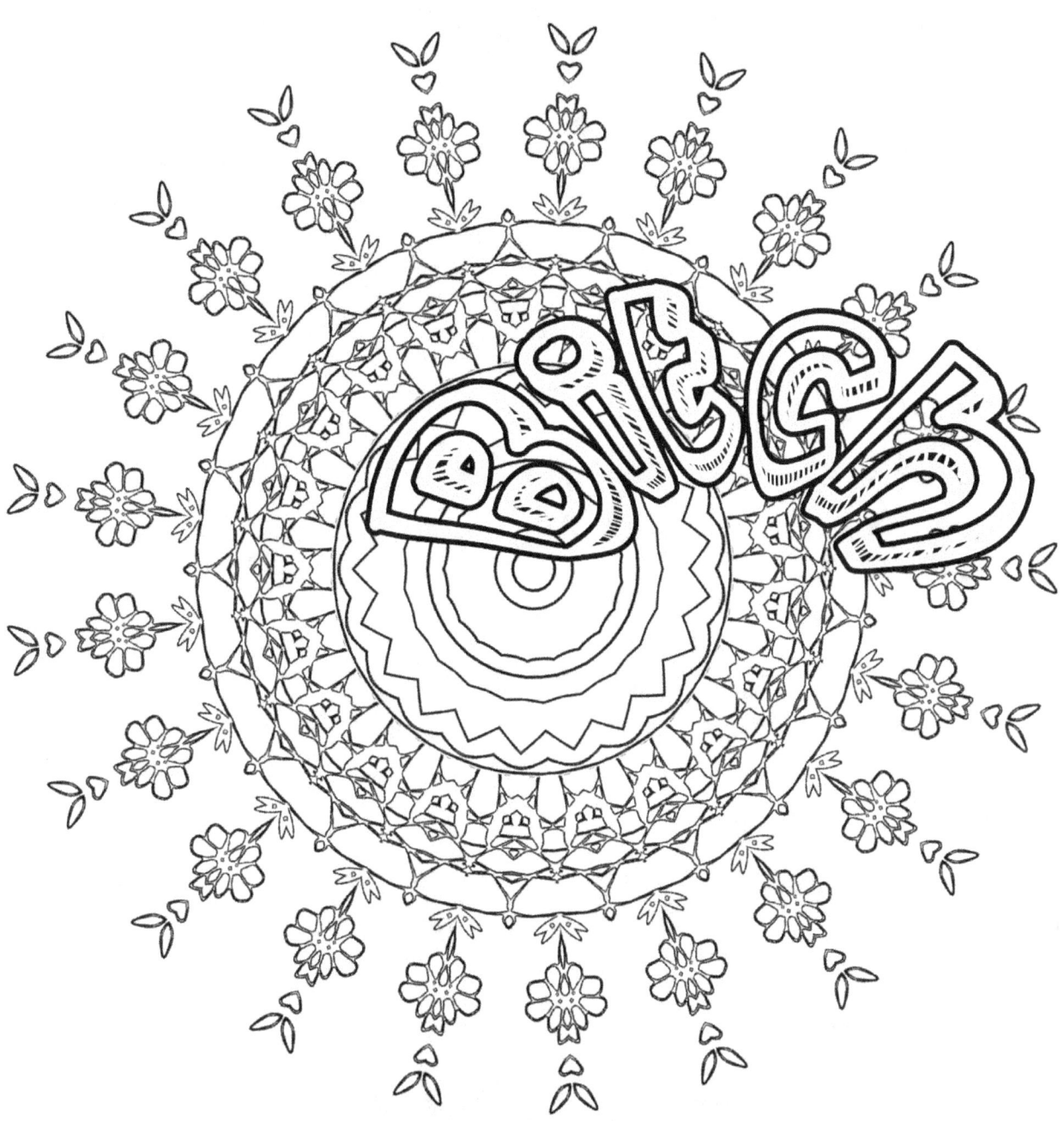

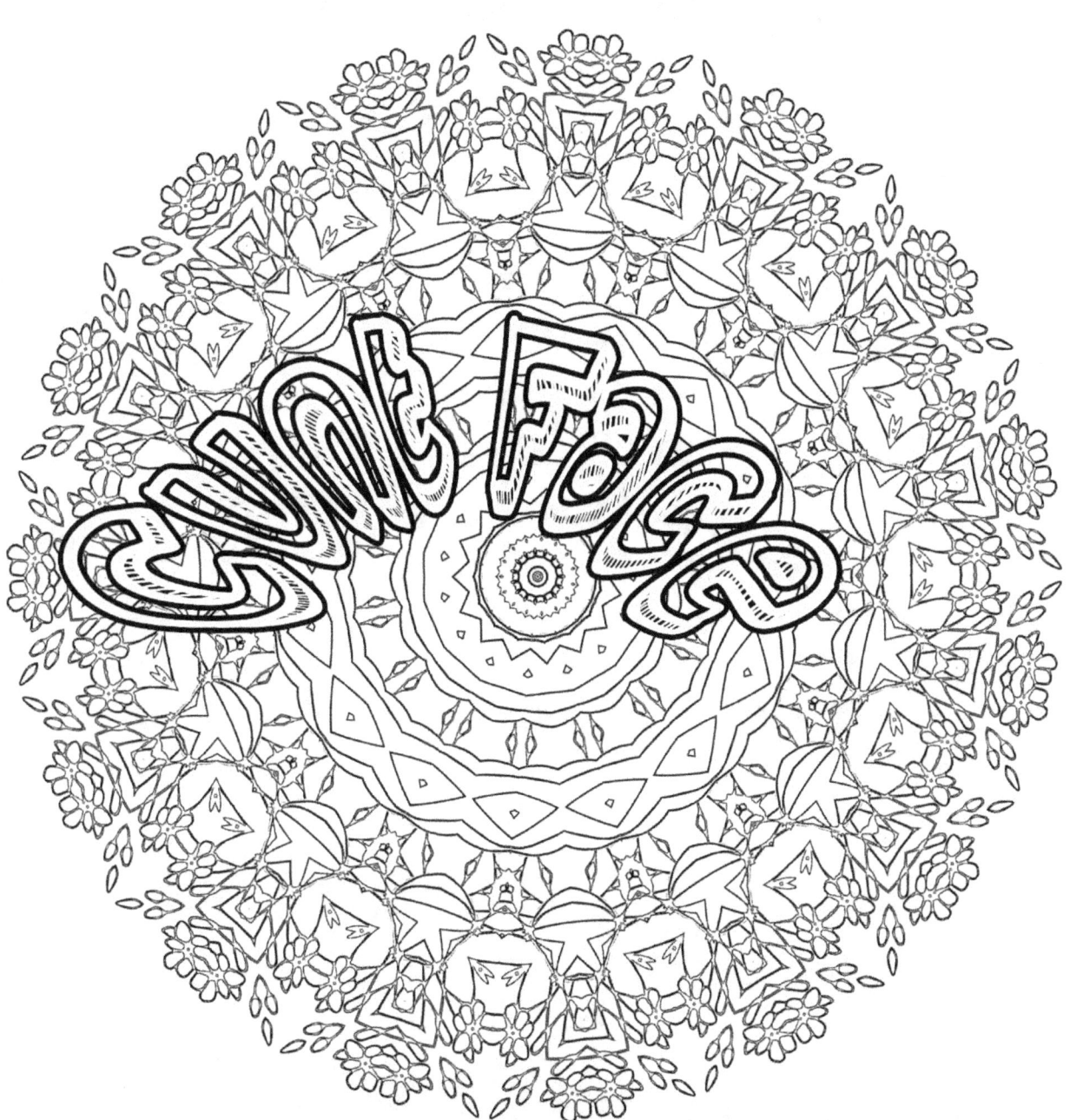

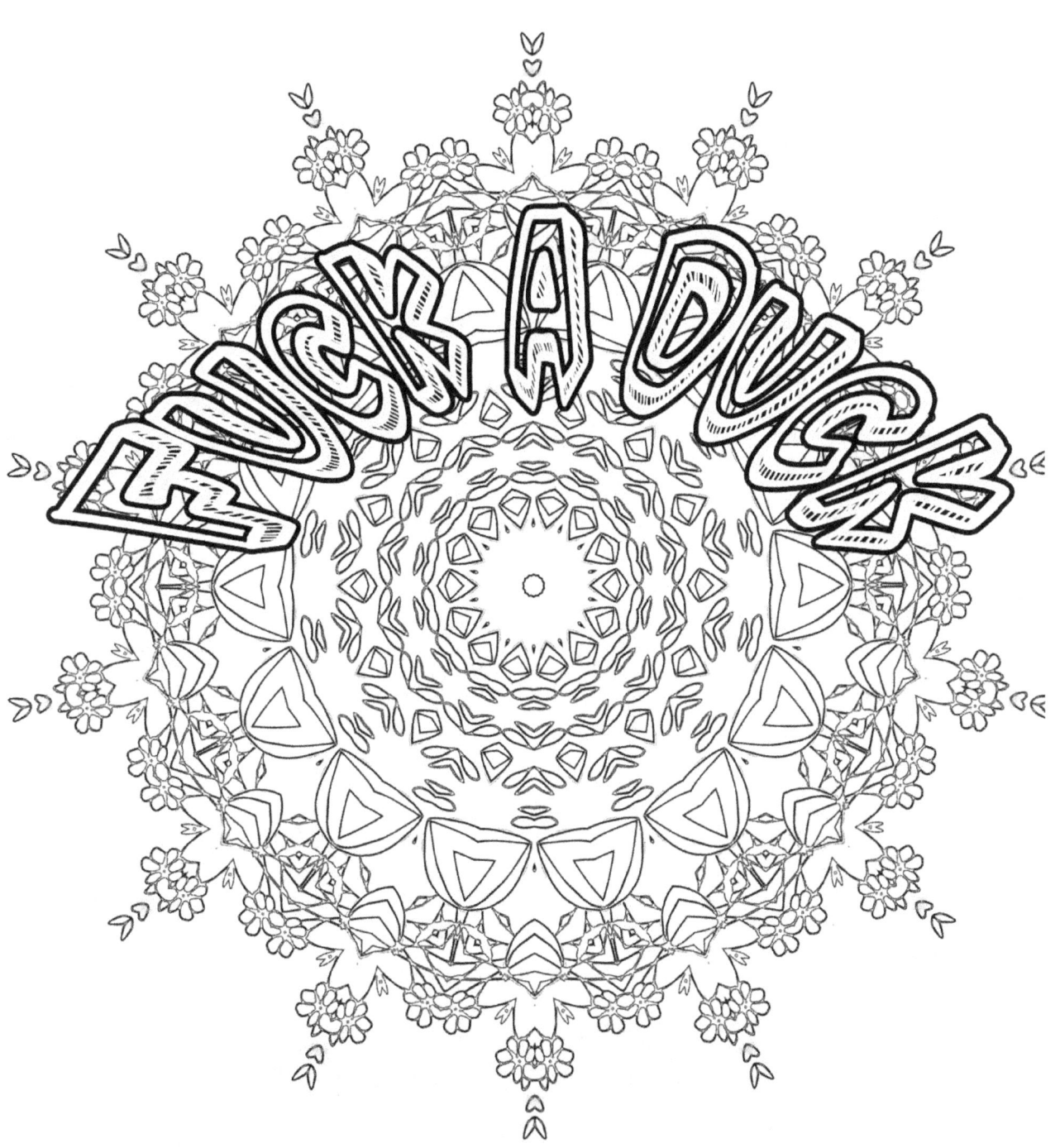

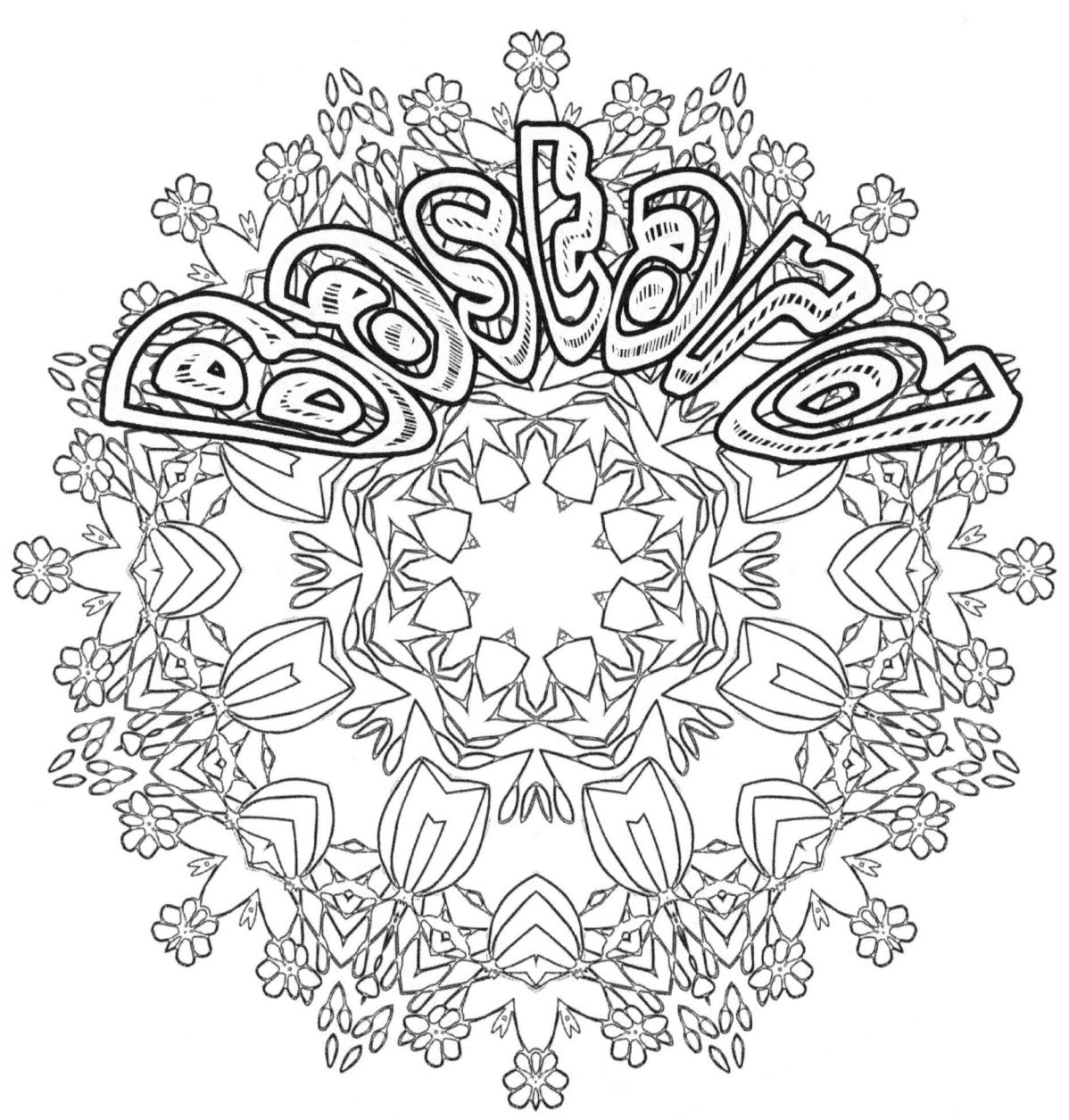

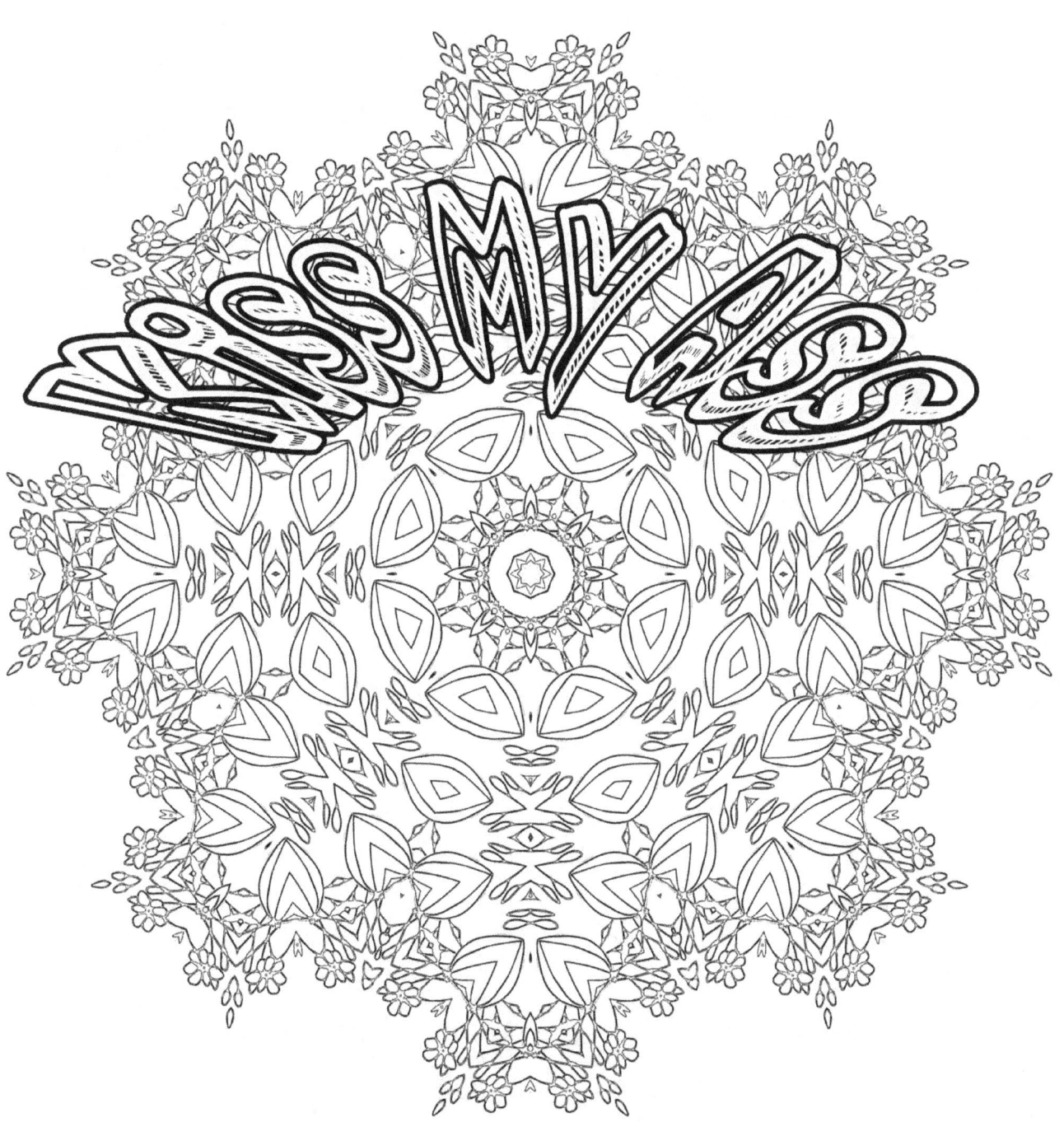

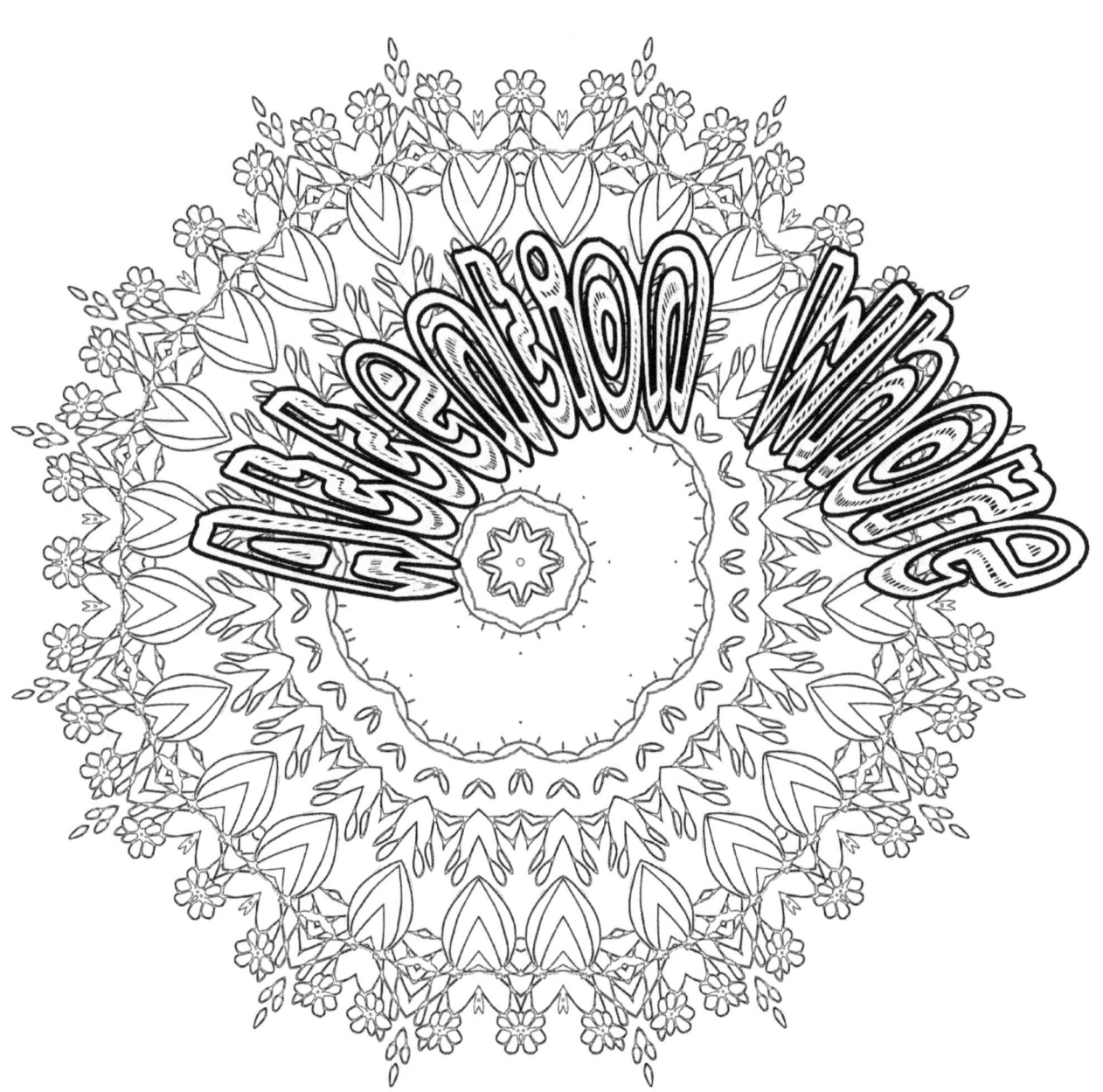

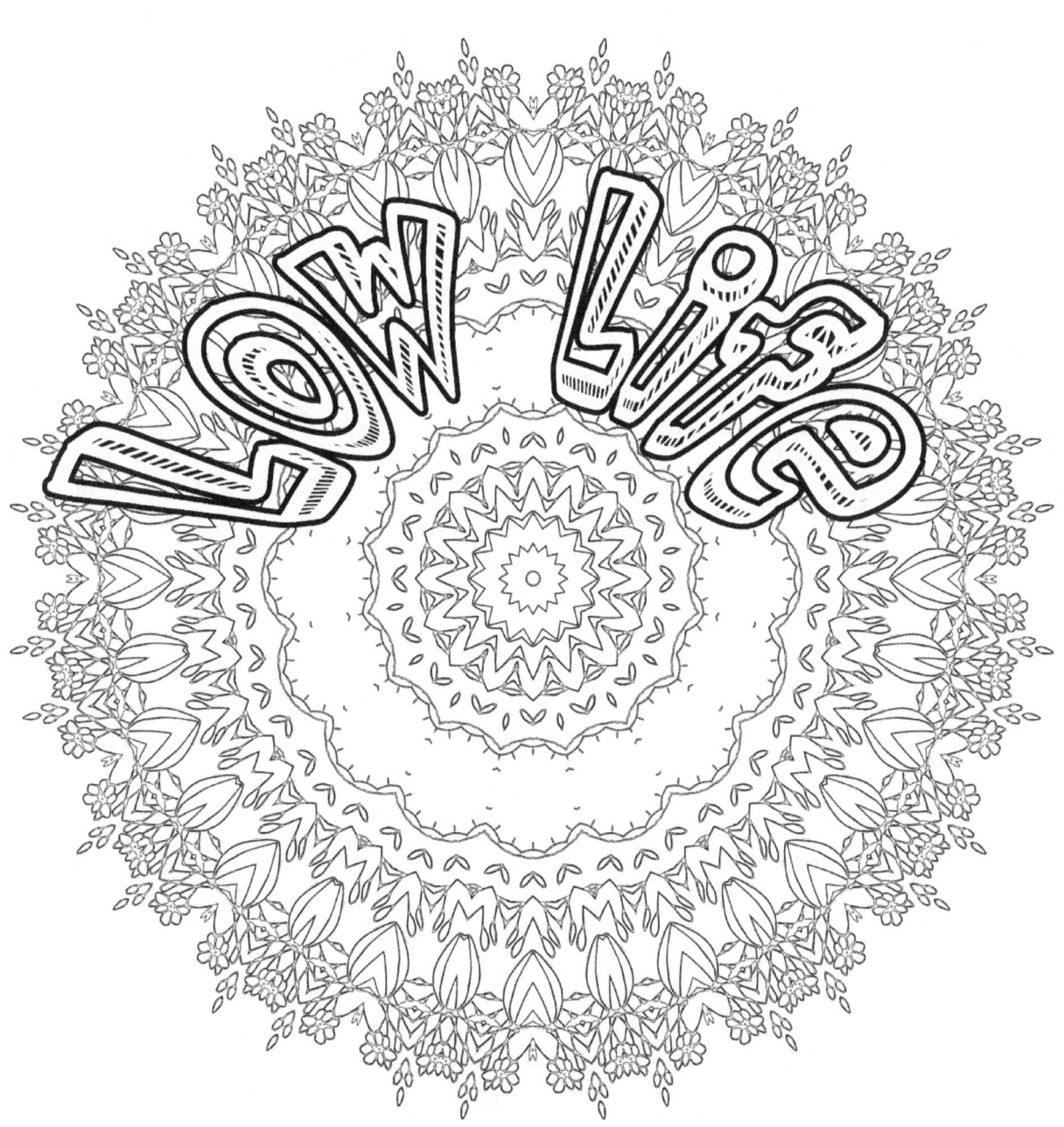

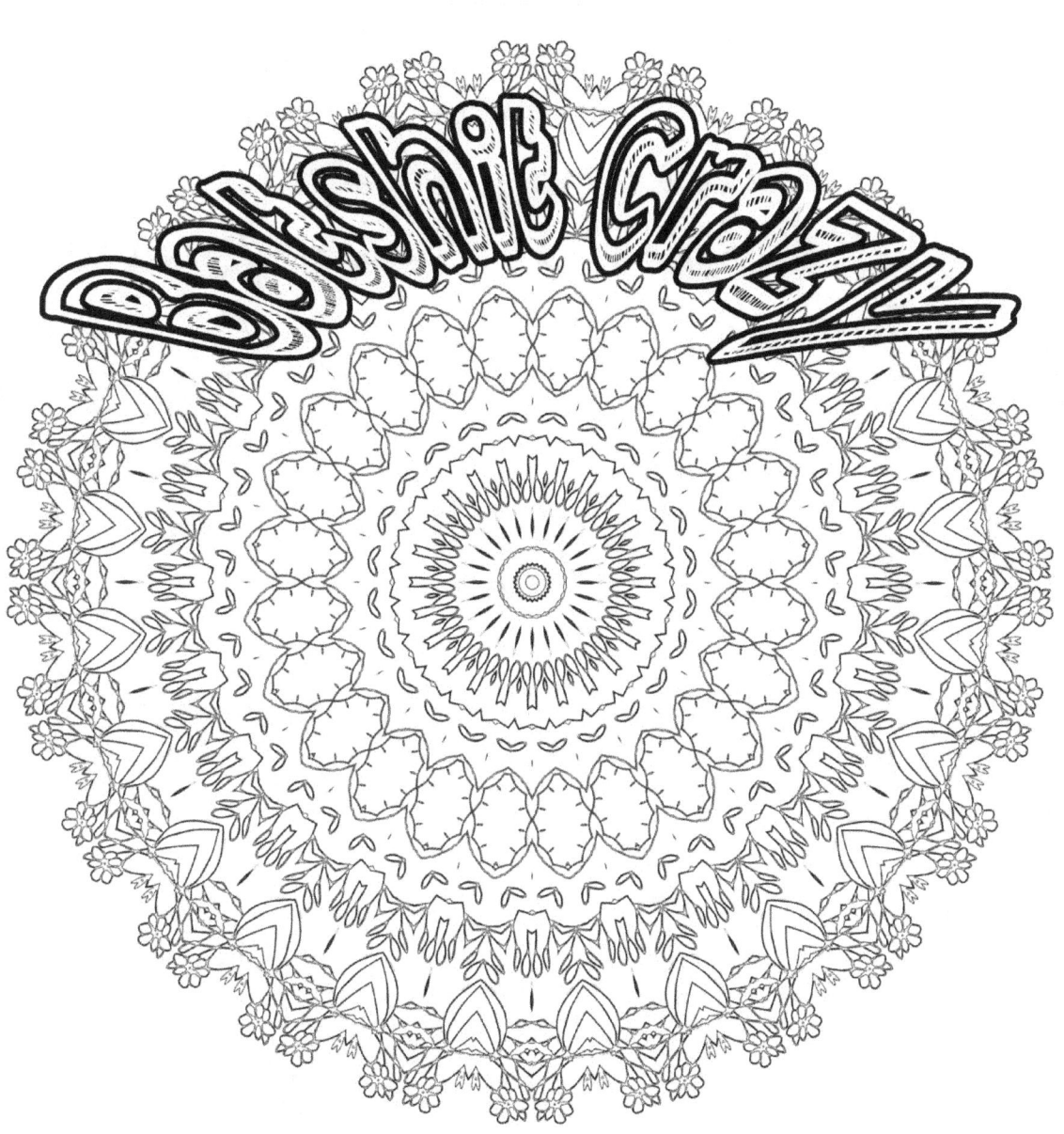

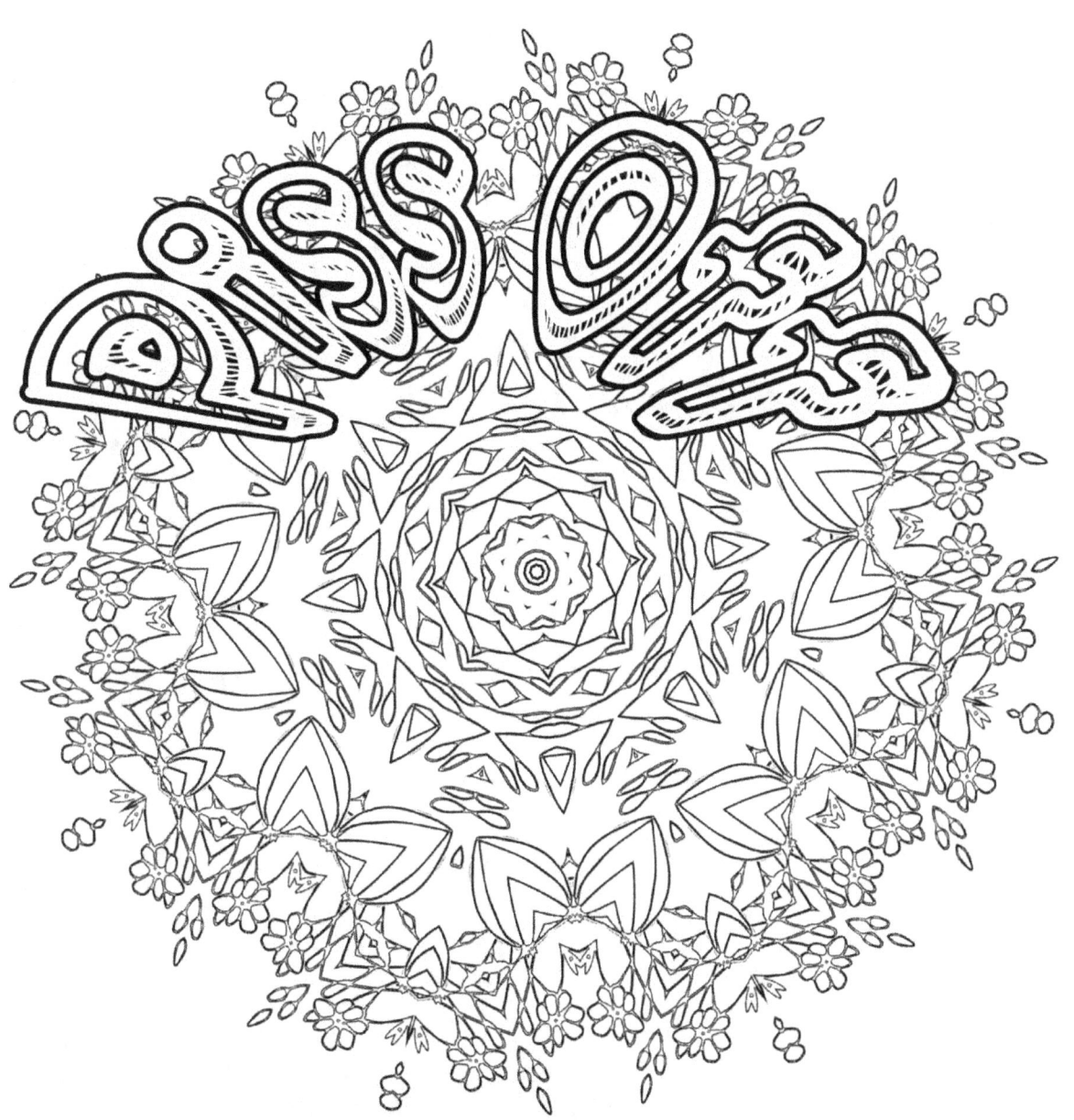

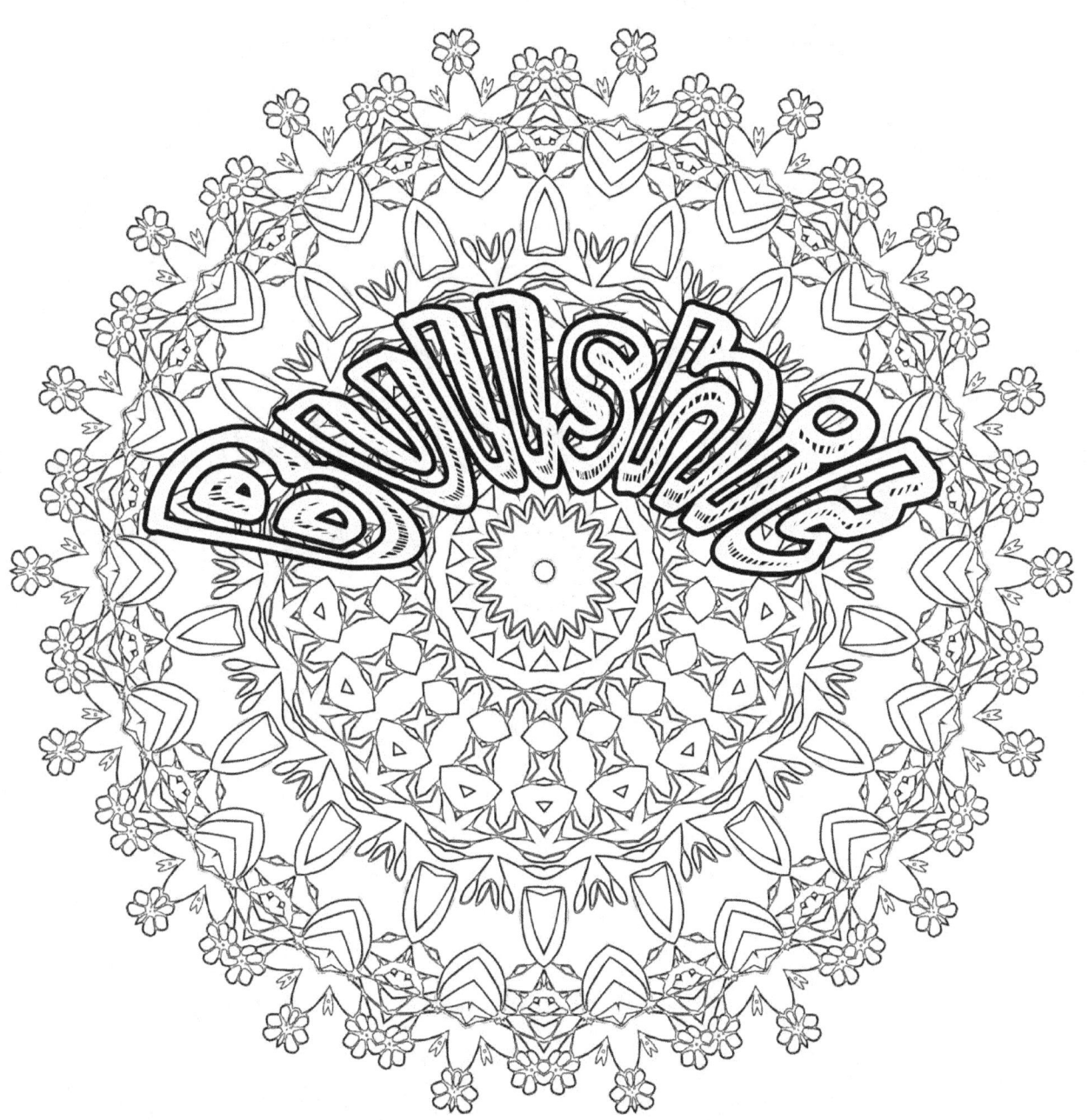

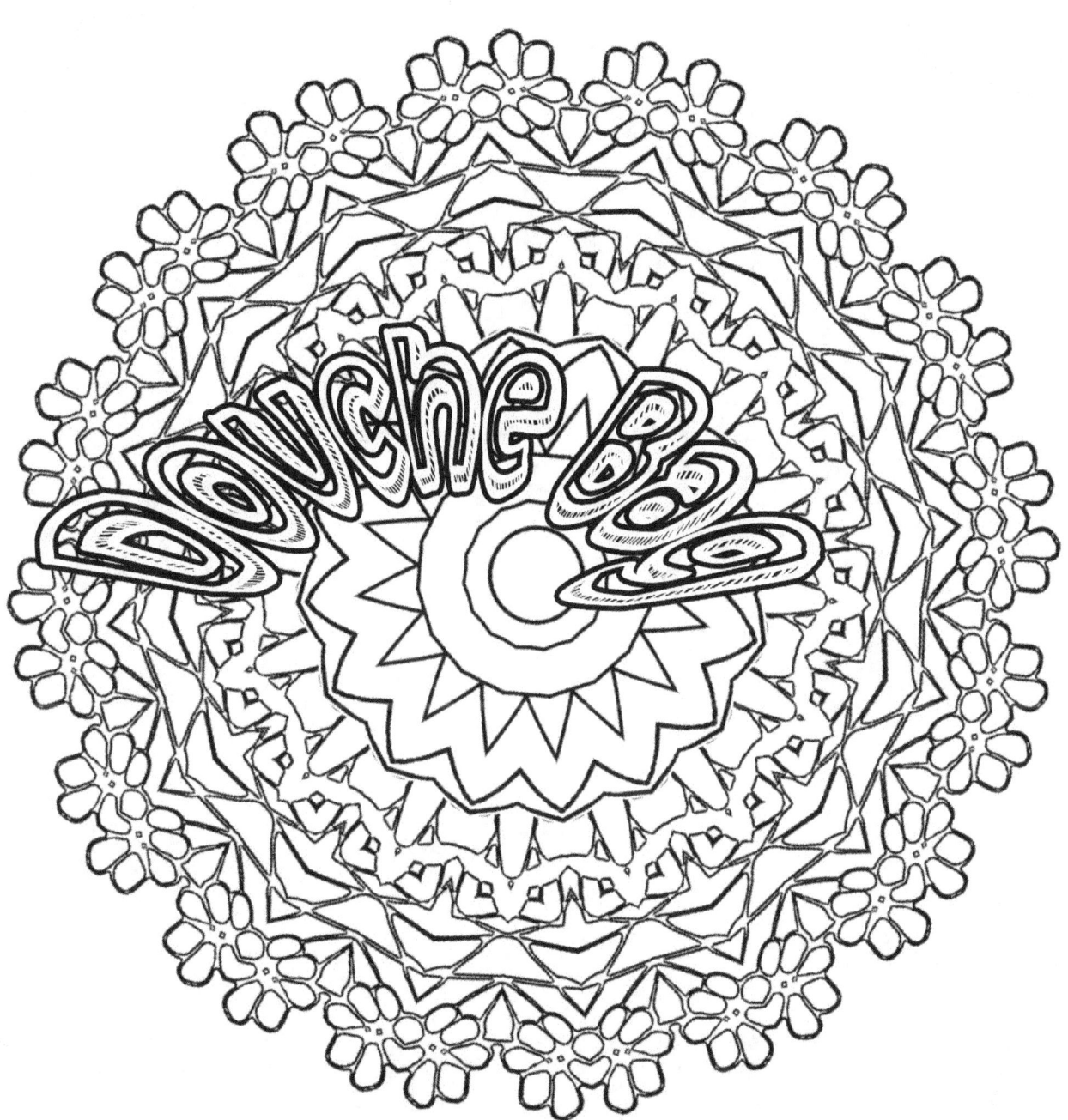

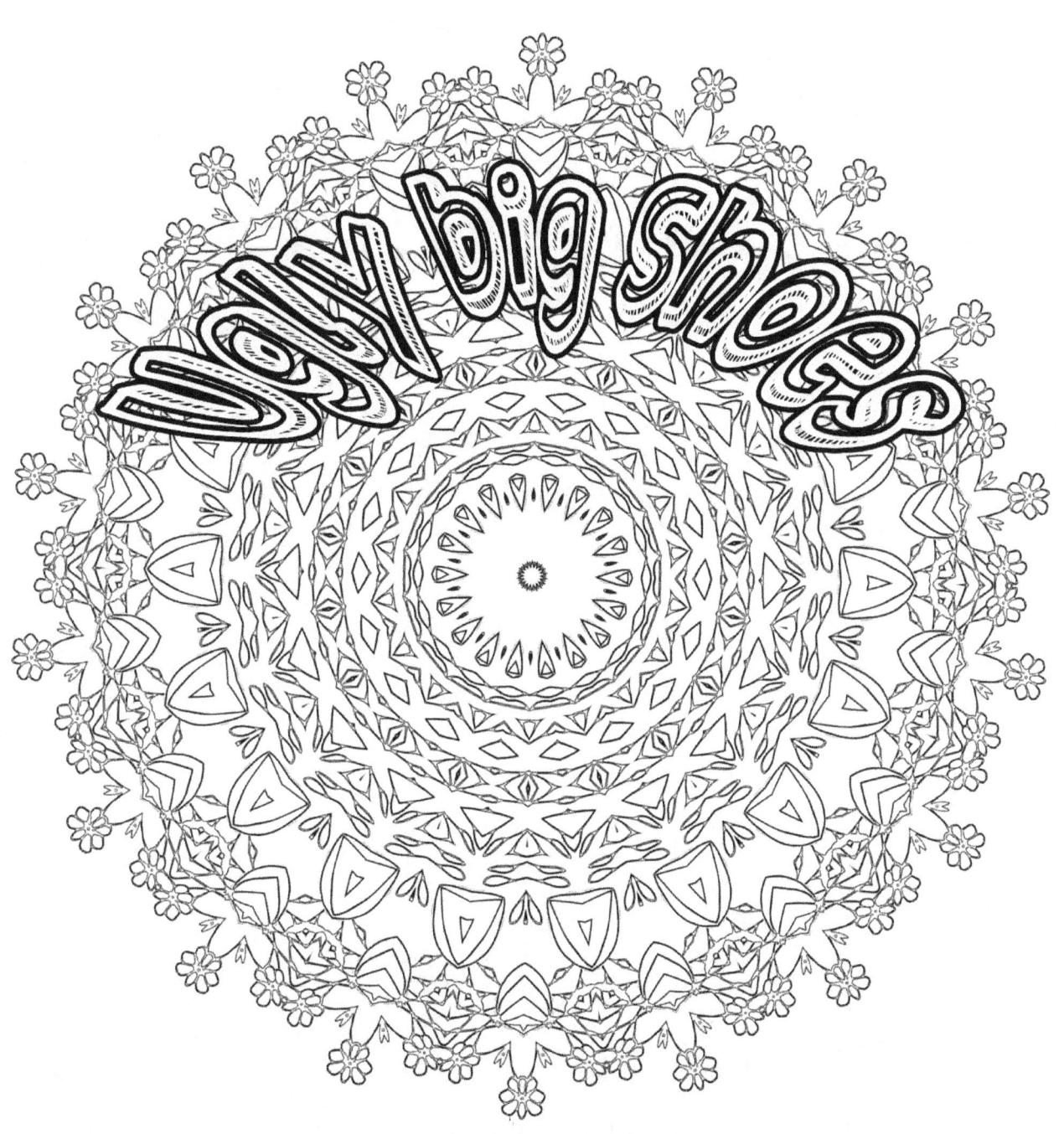

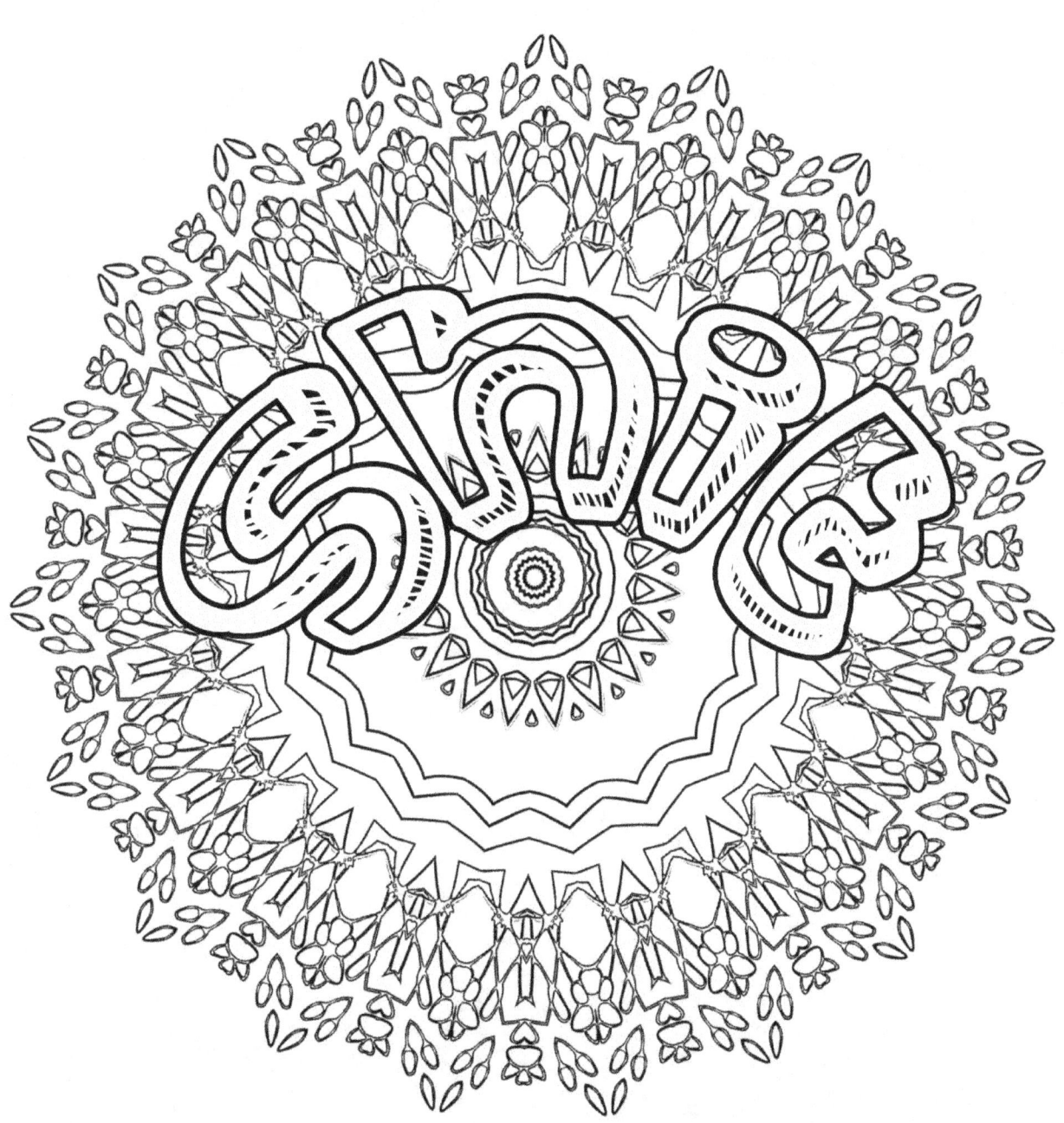

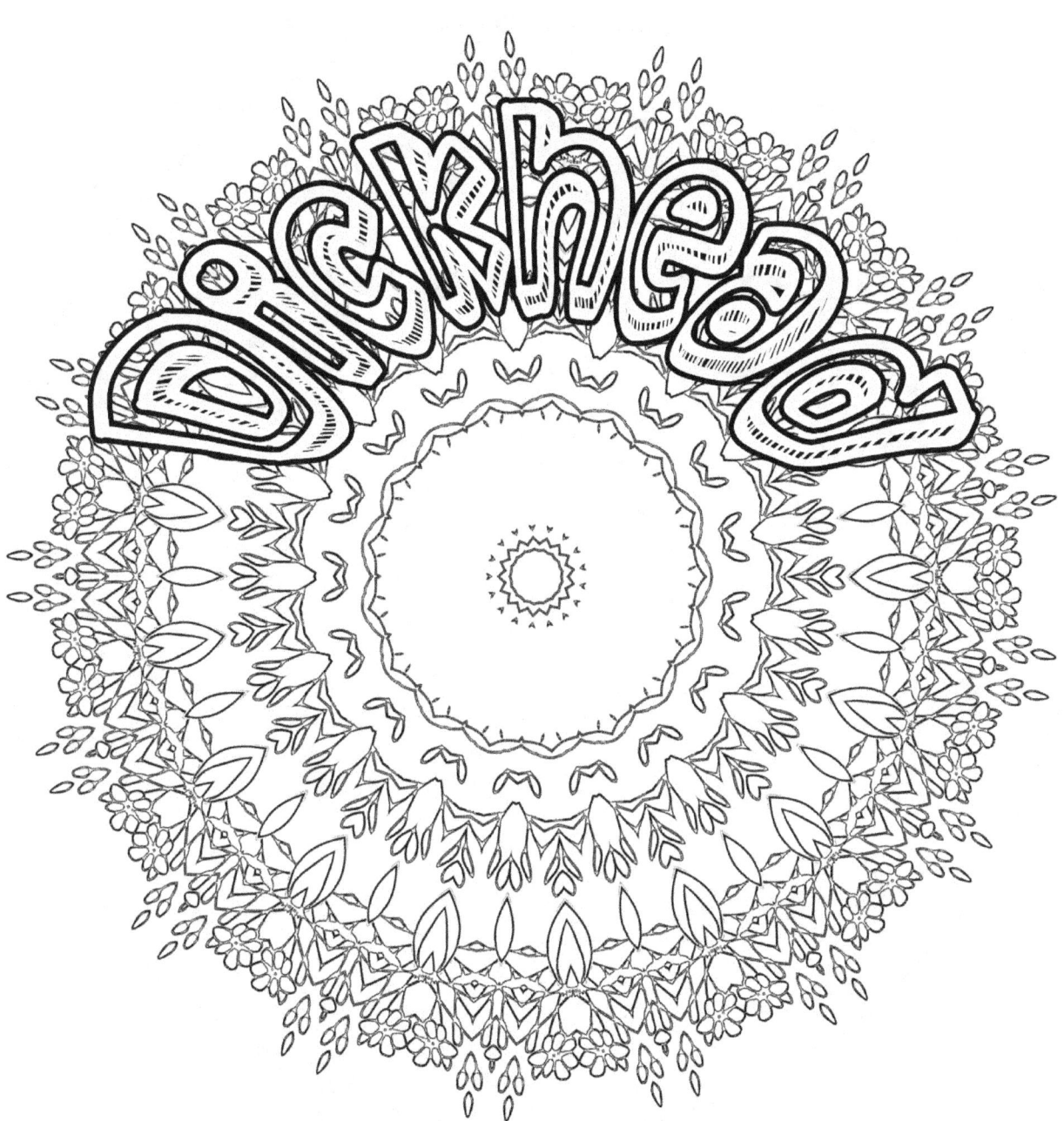

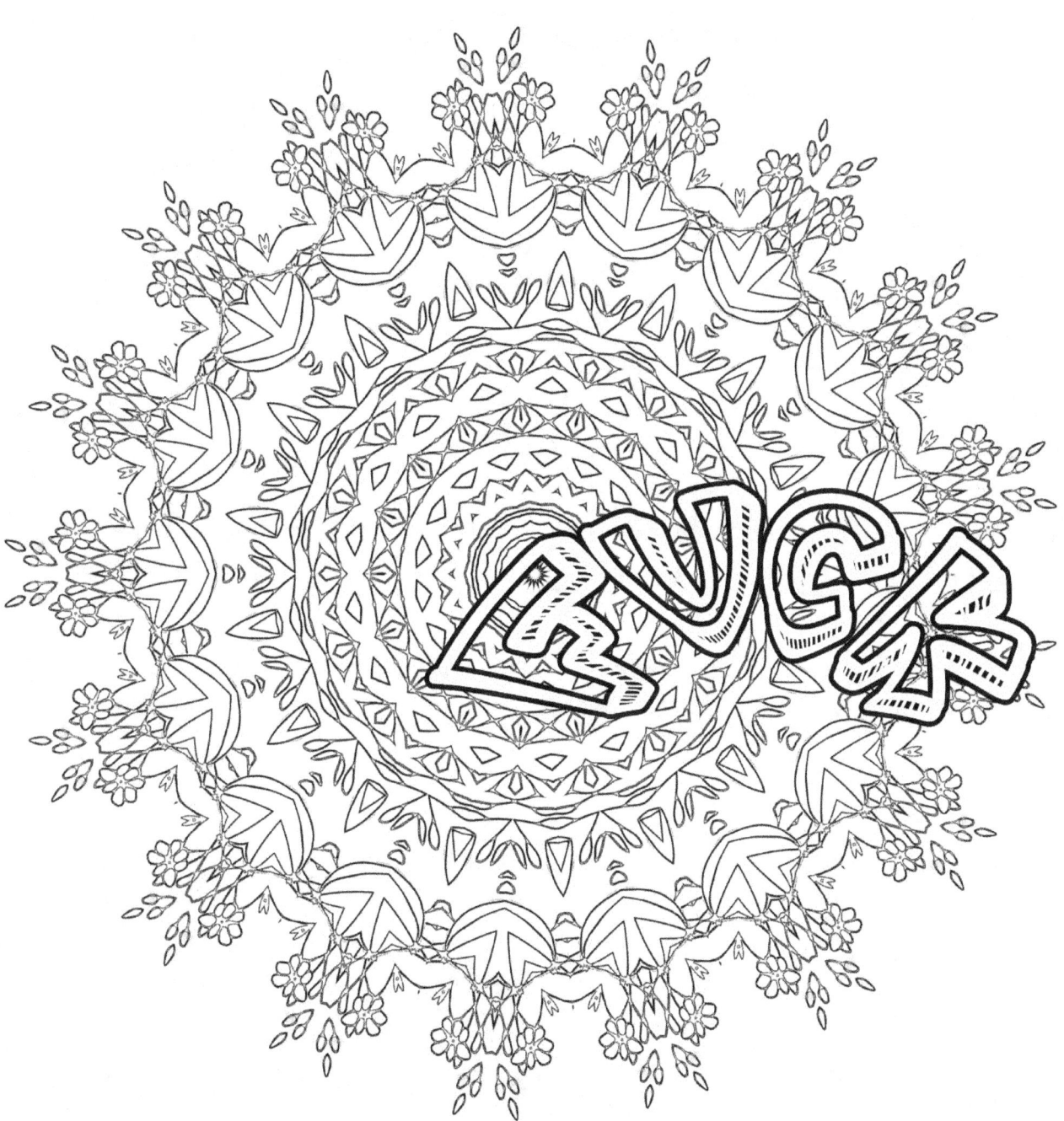

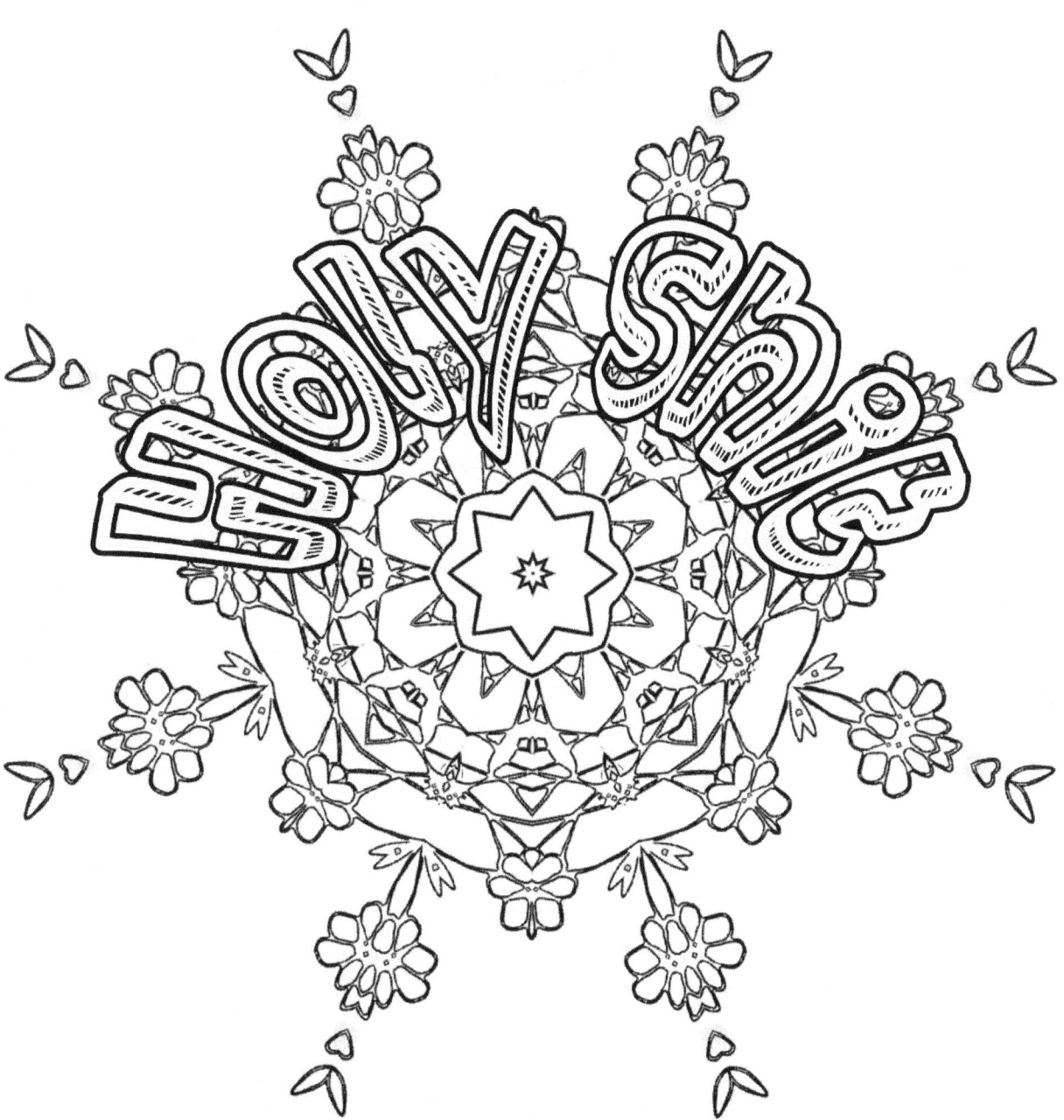

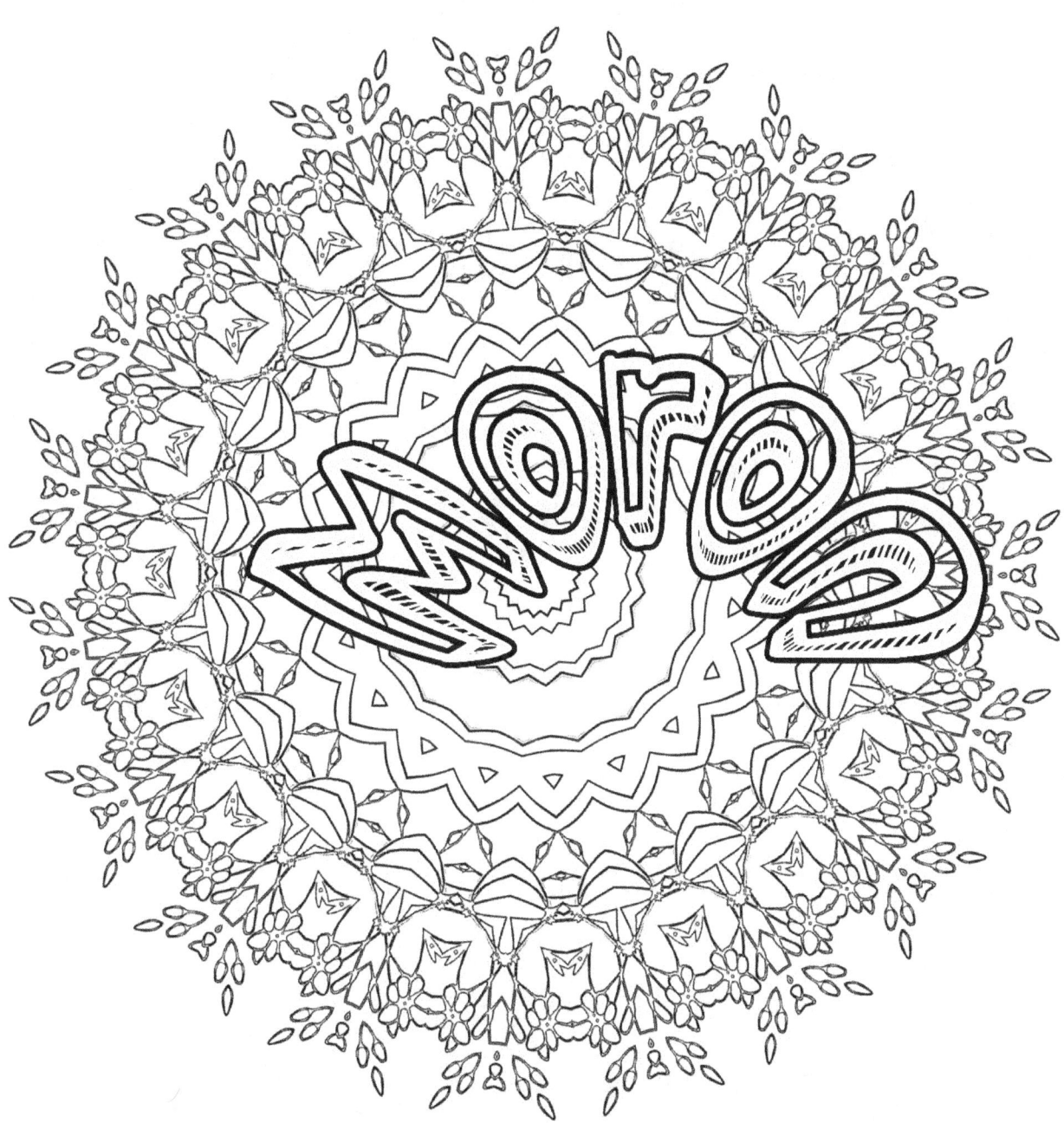

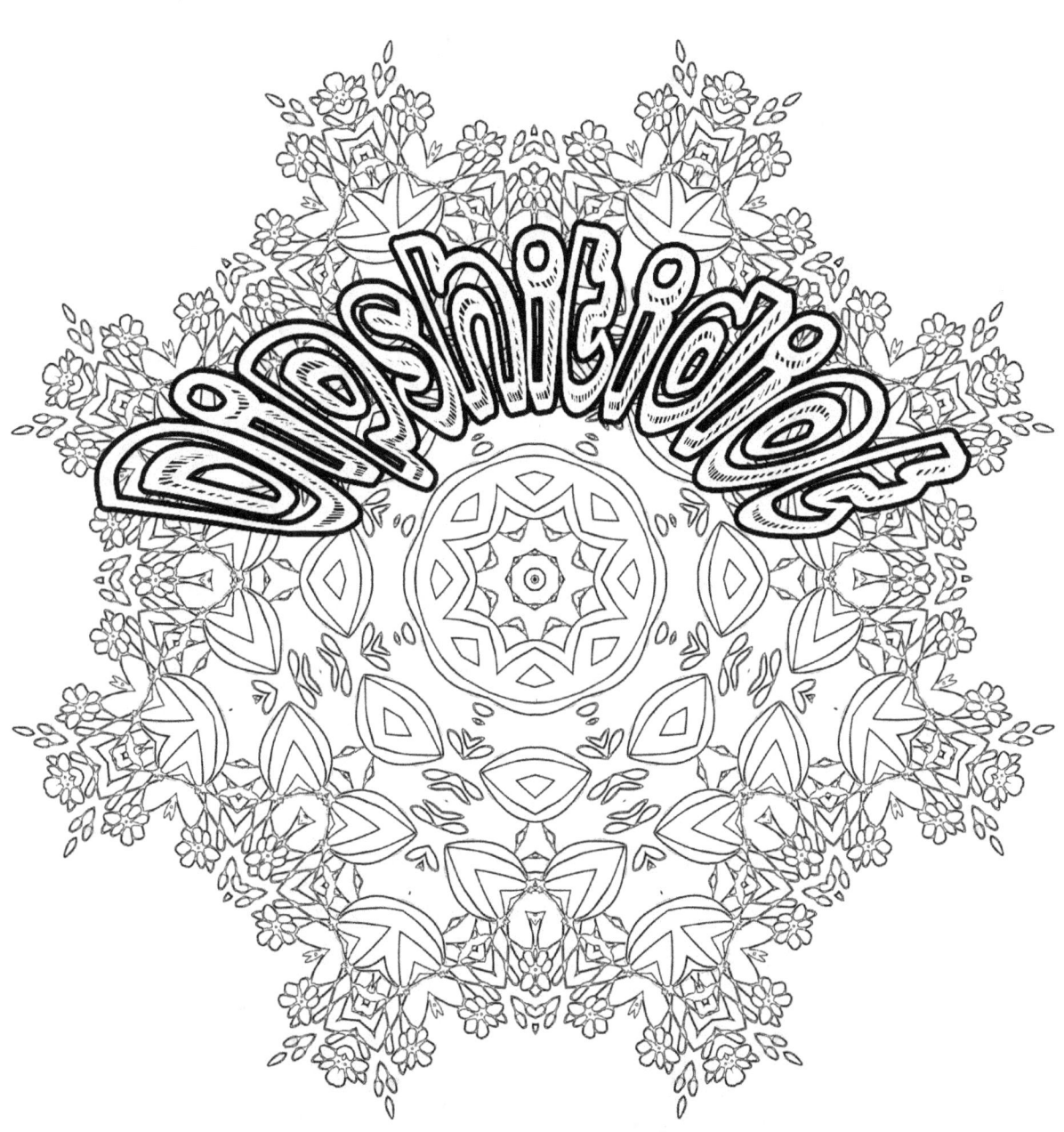

www.ingramcontent.com/pod-product-compliance
Lightning Source LLC
Chambersburg PA
CBHW081750170526
45167CB00009B/3984